Dedicated to the 95 human beings killed by the Oakland Police Department, the California Highway Patrol, and the BART Police in Oakland, California from 1970 onwards. Of 83 victims: 81, or 99%, are people of color. 58, or 76%, are black. 12, or 14%, are Latino. Between 2001-2011 the city paid $57 million to alleged victims of police abuse—the largest sum of any city in California.

"The Black Panther Party (for Self-Defense) formed in Oakland in 1966 in response to police repression. The Panthers demanded 'We Want An Immediate End To Police Brutality And Murder Of Black People.' The first issue of The Black Panther newspaper featured an investigation into the killing of Denzil Dowell by deputies in North Richmond. Oakland Police have shot and killed other young Black men like Lil Bobby Hutton (1968), Melvin Black (1979), Gary King, Jr. (2007). In Berkeley, police killed Black women like Anita Gay (2008) and Kayla Moore (2013). Earlier this year, two recent Black UC Berkeley graduates were attacked simply for 'walking while Black.' After Hurricane Katrina, 'New Orleans Police officers shot and killed survivors seeking food, shelter and water.' "

–Rasheed Shabazz, The Black Record: Why we don't know how often police kill, October 20, 2014.

Manhattan my ass, you're in Oakland

Judy Juanita

my best

Judy Juanita

Manhattan my ass, you're in Oakland
COPYRIGHT © 2020 Judy Juanita
EquiDistance Press, Oakland, CA

Cover and graphic design
Harper Design Group

The author wishes to thank the artist Karen Cusolito for permission to use her sculpture in the cover art.

ISBN 978-0-9716352-7-2
Printed in the U.S.A.
July, 2020

EquiDistance Press
490 Lake Park Ave.
P.O. Box 16053
Oakland, CA 94610
whoknewyouknew@gmail.com

Table of contents

Note to my younger self

Dick don't do friendship, missy
Dick isn't a friend
Dick doesn't console
Dick is a missile. Long-range. Short-range
Remember
Think, sweetie
Missile sits in a silo in a weapons launcher
It carries a payload
Dick is not your bosom buddy
Dick is a war mongerer
Dick is a missile, one that rapes and pillages
Remember
Dick is not even a friend to its owner
Dick ain't about loyalty or comforting you
Dick doesn't give a lick about peaceful co-existence
Dick leaves bodies strewn over fields
Bloodied legs, open skulls, glazed eyes
Dick rapes women, children, men in front of women, children, and men
It's called purview
Dick doesn't make babies. It doesn't even make sperm
Dick shoots sperm
Think, sweetie
Did Dick take your prenatal vitamins?
Did Dick's ankles swell in the last month?
Is Dick walking around with stretch marks?
Dick is a surface-to-surface missile waiting for
General Big Bubba Tubba to give it the go
Dick aims to cover the distance between your lady parts
And your beating heart
Here's what happens when missile hits target:
Explosion. Not a pretty sight
Dick is to friendship as Putin is to Trump,

Dick being the operative word
Dick made this country and don't you forget it
Dick-on-a-stick, otherwise known as gun, killed the buffaloes
In a bid to extinguish the Indians
Dick enslaved the Africans
Dick ain't nobody's friend

And here you thought Dick was a night out,
A few drinks and a friendly fuck
Not so
Every conquest Dick makes is a giant step for mankind
And that's a misnomer
Dick doesn't do kind
Dick does war. Dick wants the Middle East now
Dick is about override
Dick-ocracy. Dick-attitude. Dick-atrocity
Dick wants women in veils and out of cars
If women who think they're free really saw
Dick ravishing choir boys in supine splendor
Pushing grieving widows onto their husbands' funeral pyres
We would abhor every single acquiescence the world over
And Dick would die on the spot
Shrivel smaller than Harvey Weinstein's mogul-dick
Die, Dick, die
Die, even the proxy dildo Dick, die
Silence, quell, stop, Dick, stop it
Don't get pious about Donald Trump
He's one Dick in a billion
Women of the world, unite
Lysistrata is postmodern revolution
Lysistrata is a dick destroyer
Lysistrata is universal antidote

Let's make Lysistrata a verb
The way O.J. became a verb (He O.J.-ed her)
She Lysistrata-ed Dick
With the weapon at her disposal

Reverse the tactic. Like the pitiable girl in "Schindler's List" calling out
Goodbye Jew. Goodbye Jew
A worst example of learned hatred
Instead we take that spleen and call Dick out:
Goodbye Dick, Goodbye hard violent Dick
Goodbye, you son of a Dick

We should all be so disgusted by this perversity
That we boycott the Academy Awards or the Golden Globes
As the pimps and hos conventions they are
Orchestrated by clones of the ones who acquitted Trump
We should stop their obscene sexual Congress
Dick to Dick to Dick to Dick to Dick to Dick
Stop watching the nubile bodies they peed and shat upon

We should be so horrified that we can't bear the sight of Dick
The hypocrisy of the lot of them, the ones who knew
The ones who looked the other way

Dick is not your friend, sweetie
Dick doesn't need your nectar
Dick craves aspiration. Yours
Uses it until it asphyxiates on it

Love alone conquers this hardness
Deep in the heart where–dickless, soft,
Alive and responsive to ourselves–we
Can shape a world without missiles,

Drones, assault rifles, towering
Penile-shaped skyscrapers
Waiting to be penetrated by foreign objects

This truth is yours in abundance, my dear
It can make Dick dust

I used to feed the homeless

I keep seeing Jesus
in the homeless
not the black ones
the white ones

I keep hearing him shriek
why have you made me an icon?
he hates the beautiful cathedrals
with their stained glass windows

I hear him begging for food & dignity
on Market St.
bent like a pretzel
watching himself defecate
I can't believe this nasty revolting Jesus
even though it's Xmas

I see him beat a woman
up & down Market St.
she looks like his wife
her name could be Mary

Nobody in all of downtown
San Francisco lifts a finger
I don't lift one either
because I can't buy this Jesus

I used to feed the homeless

Poem for the rest of us

Atatiana Jefferson was shot and killed by a Fort Worth police officer in
her own home 10/12/2019 while watching her 8 year old nephew

We wear a masque called freedom
But Atatiana was shot like a fugitive slave
We masquerade as upright citizens
Brave this deadly force every goddam day
Masquerade as independent thinkers
While our thoughts get shot down in the streets

We believe, like true believers, in the rule of law
The gangs in blue shoot through that too
Our red, white and blue masques say VOTER
But our ballots keep disappearing
When the ancestors greet Atatiana
They shake her alive. The masquerade is over

Faith leaders wear the masque of concern
But their brand-new bibles are warped and cracking
Atatiana's neighbor, in masque, cries out
They had no reason to come with guns drawn.
The ancestors ask: Is each player behind the masque numb?
Some, not all, though in costume, torn and dirtied, know

The great pantomime and our long drawn out performance
Crack and peel with every gun drawn and each bullet fired

Manhattan my ass, you're in Oakland

I drive a new friend around Oakland
She's from some place called Portland
Portland had slaves, I say-
Portland, Maine, you mean-
No. Oregon as well as Maine

It's easy to get around my fair lady of a city
My pretty pretty gritty gritty city
Curled around its man-made lake

My city will not become The White House
Where James Hoban's slaves,
Ben, Peter and David, *his* carpenters,
Someone else's bricklayers built an edifice

This temperate city, 62 degrees year round,
Will not become another San Francisco
Who, in her glory, banished the people who built her

Oregon used exclusion laws
In the 1840s and 1850s
To keep free negroes out and dared
The ones there to leave at once or else
San Francisco used the laws of avarice
And greed to build its white houses while
Middle class blacks and the working poor
Who never knew they were equally unequal
Left through the same back door

I drive my friend to Oakland's shopping hubs -
From Jack London Square to Chinatown
From Old Oakland to Uptown
Hey look, a freebie bus from dawn to dusk!

From Laurel to Fruitvale to Montclair Village
Piedmont to Grand and on to Temescal

When we drive through Rockridge District, she's
astonished. "This isn't Oakland. It's Berkeley."
No, it pretends it's Berkeley
And keeps its blacks behind the counters

I show her the back doors to the freeways
The secret to getting anywhere here
in fifteen minutes tops

"We built this city on rock and roll"
Nice try, Jefferson Starship
But you left out The Fillmore
Bobby Blue Bland, Bop City
Sugar Pie De Santos doing the splits

Oh, baby, those splits built these cities
So you're not coming to Oakland
And tearing down our spirit
Manhattan my ass
Brooklyn my ass
Oakland is not the new San Francisco
No matter how many of us you displace

My friend, you said at brunch
You jetted here to work at Genentech
Jazz, the blues and my parents came
The same way riding the Santa Fe
If we needed her bus fare for lunch
My mother walked from East Oakland
To the Naval Supply at dawn

Seven miles from E.14th to Seventh St.
I said she gave us her car fare for lunch
My devout Christian mother who didn't
Allow alcohol or swearing in her house
Walked past Esther's Orbit Room
And Slim Jenkins Supper Club
Cared not a whit for John Lee Hooker
But knew the hookers on the street
Were blessed angels at her feet

To whom does Oakland belong?
The deer in the foothills?
The fauna in the ponds?
Don Peralta's descendants?
My mom and pop whose plots
Sit silent in the wind?
The Hokan and Penutian hunting turtles and deer?
Do the dead Chumash own Santa Barbara
Or do Oprah and Jeff Bridges?

I want to coexist
I love to coexist
I live for my city's turquoise sunsets
Its rainbow of tongues
Its unspoiled immigrants
Their dreams as mangled as our schools
These problems we keep working
our darnedest to resolve...

One more tip, my darling dear:
Don't take the wrong freeway exit
Manhattan my ass, you're in Oakland

People Think, Yeah, They Think

People think I'm stupid cuz I'm silent
It's all going in
It's all going in

People think I'm broke cuz I'm so damn poor
patch in the road
middling patch in the road

People call me gay cuz I love my friends to death
That ain't an insult
You think you're insulting me
For living honorably?
Praise to my ears Praise to my ears

A lady at the Arco asks for spare change
When I put four dollars in her hand
My grandson asks me why
There but for the grace... go I
This country's not a no man's land
It's mine It's all mine

An old friend called me delusional
I think she meant unsuitable
for speaking hard truth in a stately place

I love the lives I've seen
The places I've been
And my black self is too old
To hold this common knowledge in

Laborers Day, 2016

For the porter
Who shined my shoes
Let us march on

For the singer who got the lap band
And died but held the note to the end
Let us march on

For the woman trucker
Who fed and clothed her kids
Honor the grannie who watched them
Paid in hugs

For the busker dependent
On the kindness of strangers
Keep crisp bills on hand

For the factory worker in Beijing
Gluing our sneakers and cellphones
Bless the work Curse the system

For the blues lady too arthritic and stooped
To sing even at the senior center
Love only love

For the teacher's aide who loved
Those bad kids into goodness
Safe passage home

For my manicurists from Vietnam
Treated shabbily by sistahs whose folks
Were treated shabbily not so long ago
Kindness is a way of life

For the sales clerk with a short temper
Minimum wage and how about health care?

For the seamstress in a Chinatown sweat shop
Who cannot open the window of freedom
We have to open it for her
Not just buy her wares

For the phlebotomist at the hospital
Counting the days to retirement
Hang tight, bro

For his theoretical kid
My kid your kid everybody's kid
Journeying to the unpredicted future
Hang even tighter

For the tented people sleeping
Under the freeways
Working harder than everybody
(Everybody!)
To keep dignity hope love tenderness
Alive

Let us labor Let us work Let us strive
To vote To legislate To make home happen
For everybody
Let us start seeing beyond
Jobs that will never come back
Technology killing economy
Let us return To music To art
To dance To sculpture To architecture
To faith in human goodness

To hope To each other
Let's look up from our mobiles
And return To each other

A Prettyman's a Funny Thing

Hope she was good *to* ya
Cuz it ain't been good *for* ya

Hope it was good, good loving
But love's a funny thing
Make a dog meow kitty kat bark
Make winter look like spring

I know bout good intentions
But she's enjoying a you and another
You and yet another
Insatiable Insatiable Insanely Insatiable

Like that stupid man
In the muddy swamp
Got hisself in a roach-eating contest
Uh huh uh huh, roaches, baby
Crunching those suckers down
One-by-one at first
Chugged em down his throat
Like potato chips and thirst
Roaches ain't pretty but they smart
Ain't on nobody's food chart
Uh, they choked his ass to death!
What else did he expect?

Hope it was good to you
So pretty and so damn smart
To end up trapped inside
a cock-a-roach's heart

Yeah, I said it, inside a cockroach heart

My Romance, My Funny Valentine

You didn't need a woman
With an independent streak
You needed a robot
To trail you week by week
You needed a prop
Front and center at your shows
Not a quirky woman with highs and lows

You said your mother pressed your shirts
Without starch because it chafed your skin
That was the language of love
She taught you as a boy

You sit on your drum stool
Your throne, the stage your kingdom
You didn't need to make whoopee
You needed a functioning groupie
(bitter, a bit, yes, I am)

The wives aren't at the shows
Another rule I didn't know
They're like upright pianos
Sitting at home paying the bills
While the girlfriends move their tails
James Brown wrote, "The road kills"
He meant a car sliding off a snowy road
into a ravine, Ricky Nelson's plane landing on fire
The doors jam and everyone dies... those kind of
Mishaps... That's what I thought he meant

A musician's life looks sublime
Not like a trucker's, full of dirt and grime
But I got it all wrong

You needed a woman who could find
The nearest laundromat
Not Wonder Woman, sexy and strong
Washerwoman with quarters
I got it oh so wrong

You didn't want all of me
I couldn't take all of you
You were never going to leave
Your throne for an imaginary home
I needed fantasy, boo
You needed to be on time

My romance, my funny valentine
I wanted to be a golden note
A muse, a pretend wife
But muses and notes vanish
After they spring to life

And when the show is over
The cords of your arms
Pulse with a shaman's spirit
Your neck red from the sun
Of the open air pavilion

You pack your drum sticks
With loving care
Your mystic touch
Heavier than an herbal mix
Healing the audience
The bartenders
The promoters
The band

The waitstaff
Healing women ogling your perfect posture
Men too who ogle your legs pumping the hi-hat

My romance, my funny valentine
My fly-me-to-the-moon fantasy
That bass pedal serviced a fine romance
But then you set your jaw and vanished
And I banished your tight lipped face
The very thought of you
The rawhide beneath your thumbs
Your faithful drum

Banished it all
The romance
The quirky valentine
My romance
My romance
My funny valentine

THUMP THUMP: a blues lyric

When I hear that sound
It knocks me down
And I'm flat on my back
> THUMP THUMP

> THUMP THUMP

Cuz I know, baby, you been out tipping
Making something on the side
I ain't got a right to be tripping
But when I hear that sound
It knocks me down
> THUMP THUMP

> THUMP THUMP

You park and lock my raggedy Benz
Did you get even one gentlemens?
Ladies and gentlemen Ladies and gentlemen
Rhymes with cinnamon
I used to be that ginnamon
Came back from Iraq
Half man half maniac
How much lower can I go?
I can't hear that sound
Without it getting me down
> THUMP THUMP

> THUMP THUMP

With me without me you got a trainload of ordeals
But when you walk through that kitchen
And I hear your glitter heels
Dropping one by one

THUMP THUMP

THUMP THUMP
Oh baby, oh baby, I gotta man up while you creep?
We used to love each other to sleep way way back
We used to love each other to sleep way way back

A place called California

                    the golden

                                                    sun
                            works over
            time

glorious produce   a riot of rice strawberries walnuts people and tomatoes
rubus ideaus peppers pesticides people carrots unsold apricots kiwifruit
cucumbers santana   lettuce medfly larva watermelon peaches people methyl
bromide   yellow squash melons flat suburbs barrios onions persimmon
peas master plans mattachine society tangerines miwok hupa chumash
gabrielino people *fremontia californica grapes* gold plant communities insecti-
cides heydays hippies rebellion sugar beets people   ideas the glassy-winged
sharpshooters   cal tjader chinatown japantown koreatown thai town raisins
and zante currants black panthers   free breakfasts for children hilly suburbs
pomegranates people   barley oats gangs potatoes cities of refuge sly and
the family stone and the all-important *brassicas*: broccoli cauliflower cabbage
brussels sprouts and Mexico Ethiopia Colorado Brooklyn Sweden Uzbekistan
Chicago Italy Nigeria Ohio Brazil Arkansas El Salvador Singapore Mississippi
Colombia all points east north south and west spilling in and out like
hemorrhoids

Bling

somebody jumped off slave ships
                    fr this
somebody mailed himself in a box
from slavery to freedom
                    fr it
somebody else ran like hell
from the paddyrollers
                    fr it
& somebody stood up to the koo klux
                    fr it

somebody rioted fr it
somebody sang their heart out fr it
somebody blew somebody's socks off fr it
somebody blew their own brains out fr it
somebody died fr yr bling-bling

even as julian bond wrote
look at that girl shake her thing
we can't all be martin luther king
somebody fought just & unjust war
                    fr yr bling-bling
somebody died on parchman farm
at the whipping boss' hand
                    fr it
somebody became baraka ntozake
madhubuti sekou touré so you cd be
P, snoop, biggie, lil jon, lil kim,
lil slim, jeezy, uncle kracker
somebody else with perfectly decent anglo-
saxon names~fred hampton and mark clark~
died shot to death at four am fr this thing

somebody upheld our long tradition of thought
        dudley randall wrote about the melting pot:
        Shove your old pot. You can like it or not,
        I'll be just what I am
somebody died not to be called boy
their noble deaths allow you to be "big boi"
somebody bled to learn the alphabet a to z
        giving you license with all 26 letters
& the apostrophe

somebody dreamed not this dream
but a way out of nightmare
        & you wake in the middle of it–bling!
        thinking it's free and clear but things
        aren't always what they appear
somebody died a ludicrous death for ludacris to appear
        a son of emmett and ishmael recklessly
eyeballing everyone under the sun

somebody learned the dictionary from aardvark to the end
        fr yr bling
somebody's black titties suckled whomever they had to
        fr yr bling-bling
somebody played maidbutlerdummymammyconvictslave
        so you cd be marilyn monroe in blackface
        so you cd bring hollywood to the hood

bling
bling-bling

somebody gave one insignificant, unsung, whole wondrous
        life fr it

Bruno was from Brazil: a prose poem

"I'm from Oakland and I'm not a statistic. Yet. But New Year's Eve I left the Bank of America at 2:30 pm; the news that night flashed on my bank. It was the scene of the last homicide of the year, at 3:20 pm.–which meant I dodged a bullet by 45 minutes. Witnesses say two Latino males and two African-American males had a parking lot altercation. The Latino driver used an ethnic slur and one of the black guys pulled out a gun and shot him. The two blacks drove off, witnesses say, and Bruno who was from Brazil and delivered pizza, for god's sake, died on the spot... now you know the last word in the guidebook for new arrivals is nigger. And I know poor, poor Bruno heard the word a thousand times delivering those pizzas. 'Some nigguz on 90th Ave. want mushroom/salami/chicken... only nigguz want combos like that... you my nigga... when you get money from nigguz, check for counterfeit...nigguz, Bruno, watch out...' Poor Bruno, the word probably came off his tongue like spit. And he didn't know you could call a black person a nigger and get utter scorn and contempt. Like down South where they just ignored it and kept their inner dignity. But Bruno, you don't call a real nigga a nigga. That's like a death wish. Are you crazy? Suicidal? Certain words are like gods. They command respect. Nigger is a god. I'm so sorry for Bruno. He was a sacrificial lamb-that's what you have to do with gods. You have to appease them, give em a lil' somepin somepin. And I know Richard Pryor went to Africa after he made $50 million off the word and came back with religion. Stopped using the word and used crack instead. But he didn't stop folks from using it. He just made the word an academic issue: *shall we nigger; shall we not nigger*? Forget Dick Gregory's autobiography called <u>Nigger</u>. No, a Harvard law professor writes a book called <u>Nigger: The Strange Career of a Troublesome Word</u>. Nigger is a God, nigger made millions, now it has a career. And the country's leading black intellectual, a guy named Skippy, finds one of the first novels written by a black, titled, what else, <u>Our Nig</u>. So I'm proposing a constitutional amendment on the use of the word. There are simply days when it is dangerous to use the word. And one of those days is Friday night. And another of those days is Saturday night. Ok? On MLK's birthday, abstain.

Christmas, it goes without saying. The season is the reason. And proceed with caution on the Fourth of July. Fireworks, drinking and the use of the word by the wrong people don't mix."

Of course I'm African-American

When I slit the veins on my wrists in the dark of night
strange letters come out twisting and shouting
like the Isley brothers caught red-handed
in the dictionary

When I sleep I see perfect musicals
where somebody gets it right–
black people illuminated
not miscast
witty
not ridiculous
hip
not foolish
fearless
not long-suffering
kind
not compliant

Nighttime lets me know why those saints go marching in

My parents

I am old and fat and black
A simple wonderful fact

I bounced up those stairs like a helium balloon
Up. Up. Up. While they weathered the typhoon

Coon. Buffoon. Baboon. Until
they were old. And fragile as daffodils

It was structured. Awful. Simply fact
And I sit at the top. Old, fat, and black

San Pablo Avenue

Is it still the longest street in northern California? We drive down this old wide street, Oakland to Berkeley to Richmond, my father, his walker and I, out and about. It's a nice day, a good day. We pass his haunts: key club, the Hotel California where colored couldn't play, the Social Club where they did, the integrated Oaks Club. As he passes his gambling joints, a faint smile crosses his face. I wonder: is Dad ready to go?

Does he see what I see? Does he see what the pawnshop gobbled like a wolf hungry and salivating outside our door? Bicycles, the huge console television, plastic transistor radios, the iron. Does he see me heating the heavy cast iron on the stove and scorching my white blouse every time? The wolf wanted everything we could give it, just everything, even a house gambled away in all night poker

We pull up to the temple in a town beyond San Pablo. Dad chants with me at home. I want him to chant with me here. Two young men politely try to help my father when he lifts a weak leg out. As they tug him out of the car, all at once he decides he's not going. We've driven all this way, past every sordid boarded-up, closed-down, gone-to-seed, burnt-to-the-ground landmark of his gambling years. I want this redemption for him but he'll have none of it. His jaw sets and he mutters *don't push your religion down my throat*

I get bubbling boiling cauldron-in-my-chest mad. I go inside and chant while he sits in the car and listens to jazz. I want redemption all right. I want everything back. Just everything. I want the bicycles, the TV, the radios, the iron, the white blouses, and all the moments, each and every one, before the wolf began to blow the bricks to the ground

It takes awhile, but after I chant I feel better. We drive back down San Pablo Avenue. He looks around with the exact same expression, the same faint smile. We pass Golden Gate Fields, the big clock next to the freeway (post time: 1 p.m.). I slow down as we pass the grandstand. It demands that. It is empty and quiet. As we pass I can't help but hear the announcer's nasal staccato, the horses' hooves pounding the sod, the crowds jumping out of their seats, the sigh of the losers, the brash laugh, all of a kind, from the winners. I see Dad, his hair black and curly and trimmed just so, his mustache black and full. I smell his chewed-up cigar, watch him handicap the daily double and fold the racing form under his arm. As clear as the trumpet's call to the post, I hear his *hey buddy, whatcha know good*

ex-slave

massa were a kind person when he felt like it…it were his chiren who were mean as snakes… and I were a house nigga… no pribilege… you jest closer to harm… see this here disfigurity… massa's little boy was a rocking his chair… a rocking in his chair… dat was de same ole chair I rocked him… when he were a baby… and I were cleaning the floor on mah hands… and my knees… and my skirts got caught in the rocker… and I fell under de wooden curve… right under de wooden curve… and it crushed mah face… it were a broken jaw… that massa never got fixed… never took me to de doctor… never even gave a fixing for it…sally the cook gave me uh ice chunk… to put upside it… and a plate of collard greens… which I couldn't chew… but I drank de pot likker… and so mah jaw look funny … mah jaw look funny… mah jaw look funny… but all de slaves had somepin like that… so nobody paid it any mind… but after de slavery I moved to de up nort… then I walked down de street… people stare at mah face…and turnt away… but don't bother me none… cuz it weren't mah fault… but when I read in de paper bout de plane crash… oh we was taught to read… after duh slavery… it were mah most precious thing… learning to read… and when I read about dah plane crashing out of dat sky…I say to myself… I hope massa's little boy done growed up… and caught dat plane… or his chirens on it….or they chirens on it… or somebody else's chirens on it… cuz god don't like ugly… and slavery was ugly… just as ugly as mah jaw…that broked and weren't never fixed…

ole black joe singing o.j.'s blues

no black jury gon hang
dat bighead boy
from uh just-us tree

or swing his body
for de world to see

won't run nobody outta town
joyful at de site
and stomping round

ain't seen a postcard yet
wit his bighead on it

ya wanna hang him high
you gotta dig in yer craw &
hang em high ya damn self

Back then

I can't remember the first time he smacked her
Mom's shriek meant she hit the floor

He whipped big brother in the backyard and beat sister
who fought like a man and called him nigger

She would run away often and skinpop speed
her schizophrenia sprouting like a dandelion weed

Once while we were arguing over Monopoly
Dad walked in, mad at his horse losing. Melancholy,

he snatched a broomstick and struck my back
the good girl who fixed the snacks

I see it crystal-clear
gushing up from yesteryear

In sickness and health

As I held my father's hand
his doctor catheterized him
He rallied and got better but
there is no privacy in sickness

When we revisited the stainless
steel sickroom he motioned me
to leave the room
before the procedure but

there is no privacy in sickness. Later
I helped mom, her memory going,
onto the stainless gurney, lifted her legs,
shocked at the beauty of her smooth

still black-haired crotch, at the two
who in complete and utter privacy
made me. Health is an open secret
but in sickness there is no privacy

Advice to an awfully young actor

Don't go to Hollywood, Sam
You'll miss the thawing of Lake Champlain

You can't turn into a working stiff yet
Thirteen is too young

Hollywood looks all sunlight and rising heat
and your lake an impenetrable beauty

But a lake only seems to go on forever
and in a while you'll be so handsome

My grandma Jewel married at 13
For chrissakes, she didn't know it was marriage

Her ma told her she'd be ironing shirts
Your actor friend's ma is just doing her thing

like Michael Jackson's & Mickey Rooney's mamas
But a good childhood is a gift from Mother Nature

Don't chuck it for the movies
Don't go to Hollywood, Sam
Don't get screwed out of your gift

little girl

the little girl with cardboard in her shoes
the little girl at the altar on first Sunday
who drank Welch's grape juice at communion

perhaps it shouldn't matter perhaps it should
the little girl whose mother insisted with a tug
she take communion and pray at the altar

she walked to the altar and bent her knees
gracefully so no one could see
the cardboard soles of her shoes

but the mother insisted with a pinch and the fifth
commandment (honor thy. . .) firm in her heart
that the girl bow her head like a marionette

and pray to the god which the girl extinguished later
like a flame from her aqua blue cigarette lighter…
but at that angle she tripped over the flap

and the soles were exposed and she heard titters
from the girls whose patent shoes were ever new
perhaps it shouldn't matter but perhaps it did
decades passed before she asked and mother said
because you needed God right away more than
the others you needed God and it was as if the girl

reached right then into the sky and pulled God's face
so hard it popped like a worn out rubber band
perhaps it shouldn't have mattered…but it did

Anachronism

black *mother* in your purple raincoat
with your white sneakers at the mall

odede with your dark eye circles
watching the people so on their way

black *mee-ma* with your sturdy black
purse at the bubbling fountain

norah jones sings *come away with me*
you have no away

children throw pennies in the fountain
que sera sera

you walk away from the fountain
fizzy with your history

to wait outside
where it is
after all
a beautiful day

(not) Forgotten man

Whassup, Amiri, quixotic nobody
on life's big hand. Are you a little finger yet?
A historical New Jersey atrocity
mimeographing *yugen* in a booklet?

Your honeymoon with fame lasted decades
you and Dick Gregory like opposable thumbs
working it coast to coast (though poorly paid
save the acolytes feasting on your crumbs)

You were compact but never an Everyman
You blasted the bridges between black and white
then witnessed the new century, the Taliban,
Afghanistan, still not afraid to be tagged anti-Semite

For an instant you were the black oracle at Delphi
Is that nostalgia or wisdom in your darkening eye?

Oakland

am I movie star, hero, someone famous
when my taxi pulls up? klieg lights
of six police cars, the city's finest, the black-and-whites
return me to the matrix
                    And they blame us for the wild, wild West
everything is bright even the darkness

I want hello, how are you, welcome back,
sit down, relax
                    Something in the air in California stimulates
                    the desire for freedom, April 20, 1855, writes the diarist
I cut my bangs wash my hoop de ville sit
in the nightair lost in the nightsky
goosepimply at the thought of it all -
going away, coming back,
home is where the heart is -
oblivious
to the able-bodied messengers
in jags, porsches, sterlings and benzes

                    Advice to Black Californians: Let every Colored
                    Resident of the State abandon such positions as
                    bootblack, waiters, servants, and carriers, and
                    other servile employment, and if they cannot
                    engage in trading, mechanical pursuits or farming,
                    let them pitch into mining. December 12, 1857
a pitchblack world greets me kindly
when no one else will
death is the welcome wagon
greets me. treats me. rides right through me
was mining as treacherous as trading these drugs?
death is the transaction, the good, the service

General Persifer F. Smith took off his cap
and made a profound bow to every colored man
he met in San Francisco in 1849 because, he
said, they were the only gentlemen who kept
their promise

the old folks are hard to hear. difficult to see
I have to decipher them. "I was living in the lap of luxury
and then I stood up." what lap? what luxury? who stood?
not a mile up helicopters roam restlessly

> *if you've never been to the ghetto*
> *don't ever come to the ghetto*
> *cause you wouldn't understand the ghetto*
> *so stay the f--k outa the ghetto*
> *—Naughty by Nature*

boom boxes and aftershocks have the same velocity
when I lie in bed

elementary school lesson: lockdowns
are not for languid minds. shut the doors
shush the kids. get them DOWN! the black-
and-whites chase a murder suspect through
the schoolyard

last week it was gunfire in the middle of day
from the funeral home cross the street
"how's that for punctuation?" the teacher asks
herself as she thinks of moving to atlanta
where "people still smile at you on the streets"

good will and good luck and good evening
sound about the same

firestorm comes firestorm goes
AK47 starts AK47 stops
devastation
Devastation
DEVASTATION
the devil's station
death smiles
happy to get a day's work

everything is loud even the silences

We

is *we* in the dictionary of african-american slang
or is *we* archaic?

has *we* been cut in hard edged pieces
upperlowermiddleloweruppermiddle?

is *we* is or is *we* isn't?

is *we* synonymous with our glorious past?
did *we* have a funeral and forget to come?

do *we* speak the same language?
do *we* understand the subtext

of the language spoken about us?
could the griot call out:

all black people come in come in
calling all black people come on in

and would *we* once again
come in?

Poem for my shakubuku mother

(shakubuku = to introduce another person to nam-myoho-renge-kyo)

I had no sense of being born to her
but I loved her with such passion
her armpits were my sweated second home
her clothes closets stuffed with whiffs
of estee lauder. pleats of eggshell white
she looked like my real mother
thirty years back: their large lips
ochre-beautiful petals blossoming
beneath their loopy lidded eyes

her boyfriends were my arch enemies
super scoundrels. the squirrels in her
attic bothered her infinitely more than
those roughs who walked her house
owning it and her for brief weeks-
brief, tumultuous weeks when their wet
lips bothered me, wet on mine, mine dry
how many mouths can a river have?
kitty kicked by one such tough
caused his departure. good kitty

her loosened front tooth, her cocoa-brown
neck remained. and her heated towel
rack. her burgundy towels and rugs
burgundy nub at my feet. her burgundy
tub and scale. to her house, to her house
I went. from my house from my house we
left. one sunday I cooked plum tomato-
lasagna with three kinds of cheese.
she had hot dogs on the way over. but
I was her child. for two years brief

lasagna aroma, my aroma, her own aroma
escaped her. her sense of smell gone
from flu, I had to tell her on hot days
to shower twice. spilling like peas
from a chinese pod, her womanscent,
pussy-sharp in pungent spirals, nauseated
me. made me want to protect her. her
cigarettes, caramel corn, ivory princess
phone I handed over dozens of times
I have no sense of being born to this woman,
but I loved her with this passion. she carries
a baby now. unimaginable. I was her baby
her special dripped-clean plum. rolling
in the darkness of her heart

momma love you yepper do

momma love you yepper do big ole baby boy
love to slap her red red bag of mad
against your suedesoft baby buttock

momma love you never likes to swim the Sea of Tears
find that ragged lobster claw snapcrack shell of hate
that swacks your baby bootie end to end your baby smile
to sad

momma love you little poopie even pooping in your pants
and playing till your poops hang low as fishies in a net

momma love you all the whacking slapping hitting spitting
in your sleep momma with her daddyhands her daddystrength
her daddymight makes right

momma love you even when you sang a sweetie peetie kicked
and whipped for stealing gum   in tubs you sang and whistled
like a chirp in water hot to etch your whipping twice into the nerve

momma love you yepper do watching for your footsteps
through the door fishing in yim smokesoaked redrimmed eyes

oh you smile those eyes at what they saw big ole baby boy
taking all the touching tough inside those brown big eyes

momma love you yepper do more for all the less
the switch the swack the slapcheek shriek
the speedy harsh caress

momma love you yepper do how were you to know
momma love you yepper do love you yepper do

Woman

I just want your pussy," so he said
and she presumed him better for the battering
of a 14-year bad marriage

love puddle dry
when the sun come out
woman I just want your pussy

she saw him sweeter for the souring
and kinder for the harshening
and thus hungrier for her love

heard folks marry
till death do they part
woman I just want your pussy

it seemed to go that way
until she turned a corner
and like stealth in a well-conceived plot

she came upon a thought (an infinite mistake
akin to weaving new blues
from a heart of deadred strings):

gold disappear
when the rainbow fade
woman I just want your pussy

she would be sensitive to him
and he to her and they a one
the way pop tunes say love is done

but the boy who loved his old soul crooners
sang his song from the top of his shredded lung
in a howling wolf's voice:

love puddle dry
when the sun come out
woman I just want your pussy

a white angel

a white angel
standing
on terra firma
watches us
worm our way
out of soil
so dense
we weasel
our way up
sucking the eggs
of snakes and frogs
until we dwarf him
and his black scarecrow
and the blessed cracked earth

sonnet

brothers get ferocious when they fuck
cuz bros got to represent when they fuck
they got to represent family, other black
men, your past lovers, the race, black history
they bring all this into the bed so please
do not attempt to fuck a bro on a futon
hollywood shows you how white men fuck
on tables and stairs and hard surfaces

marble staircases and walnut desktops. pullease!
to fuck a bro you need mattresses pillows
air bags sealyposturepedic waterbeds foam
and you best have a chiropractor in the next room
bros work at fucking. they may say
fuck work but they work hard at fucking

hounding tale

you never knew truth
you never made history
you never invented wonders
you never built one pyramid
you never shaped mythology
you never fashioned philosophies
you never took part in civilization
you never raised temples bounded
by granaries and slaughter-houses
you never conceived the universe
& never carried its weight
you never conquered
you never prospered
you never mastered
you never were
you never will
you never are

under-
stand?

why our bridge never went up

maybe I made up my I-just-don't-like-unhappy-people mind

unhappy sainted unhappy long-suffering noble kindweighted people
maybe we never why we got together you remind me of my mother whom
they called a black jew (and I never knew jew a backhanded compliment)
because of her crooked nose and through that same nose her sounds permeated the c.m.e. church and I was ashamed and asked her to sing softer and she
said she couldn't the lord wouldn't mind *oh how I love jesus because he first loved
me* and these songs score my erotic fantasies

maybe I thought you were she was right and I was a wrong in knowing in
my heart she loved her she-was-never-happy jesus your mouths the lips alike
uneven brave holding onto hurt for all its worth

maybe I had it you she Him them pegged wrong like when james brown
would sing scream sweat and we would grind wind scrunch and he would
say *please please please* and my noble-longsuffering-church-every-sunday-
migod-her-god-every-day-mother would come in (oh we ate god for when
wheaties ran out breakfast, garlic sausages for lunch pinto beans and god is
love over rice *please please don't go* she used only dull-edged knives – we had
sharp tempers dull knives and that was the first thing you noticed me my
sharp tongue – to cut our god who was a flour sugar salt staple)
so she would come in right on that part *please please* and she'd snatch her arm
up my record off the crack it across her thigh box all of five feet tall and sob
cry beg us saying nobody but nobody should ever have to beg anyone for
anything that hard and we'd be pissed counting money buying records for
our scrunch parties at each other like you buy it this time I told you not to
play it when she was around

and I still don't underyoustand her I never begged Him or you or any them
although the temptation like sunshine on a cloudy day was there
what can make me damn you are still in and around me feel this way

unhappy people are the sharks in the ocean of love
silent partners from the deep who play on encircle you
maybe I see too much mirror in you of her me hey man
the only boat rocked reason it's worth reflection
shark bite leg lost love deep hate float sea tide
brought it in is because I came close *please please please*
almost broke my own take don't beg record over onto up your never new
thigh please please hey man even though I still don't underyoustand her I still
have the you her all of six feet even a ghost guest in my house heart and if I
never see save you off a cross like the one she He they stayed on I'm positive
I can always hear the heard sound of your she shark bite and the felt taste of
our love lost under the bridge

always hear the heard snapped sound of your she shark bite
and tasted felt feel of our love lost under

at the cianci st. bar

for every some one
any apt body her
sweet warm kisses
at the cianci st. bar

float on the tip her aura
tonight free rash and tired
but not too
for tonight her

kisses are sweet rapt
rosé dried and warmed
by the great
falls flow

a bus ride away from
her shanty tear town
aprilshowered
with celibacy

this night her kisses
warm and winelip sweet
in early eve her
she at the bar

holds the eve
in the tip of
her budded
beer

old love

old love
when I approach you
even on paper pandora boxes
three thousand miles away
memories thrust in
to saturate my gaping
womanwound
rectifying urges surface
drown *dowopdowop* blues
I refuse him chocolate cake
infatuations transgress
saint mammy syndrome
salt pork shoppers starve
inward eyes   slow graying pubes
albert ayler recorded our song
heartloveheartlove died young
circular indecencies
exhume loud grapplings
in two family houses
our matrix held
we were synonymous
who believes it when it happens
babies scream in the night
people just want the bottle
why do I care if the sun don't shine
as long as I know he's mine
archie shepp lives on
off the radio
love plays
midcentury rage
loving eras record

paper love crumples

Thief

for Elizabeth Sarfaty

I propped this photo, your family
At the river, on my pillow

Though you went to great lengths
To explain their troubling imperfections

I see a group who fought a thousand years
Ago on a blood-besotted battlefield

And vowed to the death
To reunite in love

After my father died, I sat beside him
For two hours in the nursing home

I didn't know
That people are irreplaceable

Our family changed
We squabble more, talk less

Treasured photos disappear
We have picture-thieves among us

I have stolen this picture and will
Not return it. Thank you very much

Fragile the bond never tested by a hard pull

For Rahimah

we ate our wholewheat bread. saved the crust for each other. you and I alike.
with our thin skin. thick skulls. our kids brown and twined. like your fresh
baked. monkey bread

we clung to a Haight and Fillmore from our past. combed split ends of our
naturals. college. the sixties and Berkeley. our marriages from then. with
single stroke

we caught on slowly to Newark. to riffraff euphemism for nigger. bought
pretty prints in outlet stores. with Jewish-Italian riffraff

we knocked heads with the black elite. pulled away. we don't eat meat. you
and I. we chewed instead. on pain

I remember the nagging feeling. we hung because. it's a rare circle that opens.
that sunday set. I gave when you got your m.b.a.

I forgot Jersey's blue law. the liquor. the borrowed box took forever. to arrive.
so folks could bougaloo. you. incensed. threatened not to come. at all. they
were your friends. what the hell was I. supposed to do. with them?

it turned out all right. the music. my neighbor's wine. your girlfriend's rum.
déclassé beer. cocaine-juris doctors in the back. bid whist and weed up front.
my head high as benfrank's kite. that distinct bad taste in my mouth. when
friendship strains

The bus terminal

the missy children drop them off in compact cars
they speak a different language
of cleaning
maiding
ironing
of pleasing me missus
of washing me missus tennis whites
of me missus children home for break
and extra loads to wash

turning out her very Jamaican lip one who is young pouts
missy call her down during her favorite show
every time
will she have no peace from her missus?

rose barrette on plastic rose-colored stem sticks
in her hair
the weekend awaits its unburdening in Brooklyn

the last maid in my line my grandmother young
a chambermaid in a Muskogee hotel gingerly
picked up soiled towels shielding the pupils

of her young eyes from couples coupling uncoupling
requesting fresh white towels her daughter told
me this young
teaching me to read and read well
so I'd never have this to fall back on

The word *divorce*

at first I used *when I stopped being married*
the need to hear it anyhow
led me to a noisy apt.
smack in the center of town
where garbage trucks
throttled predawn
empty commuter
trains careened
through the night
boxcar after boxcar
vibrated the gap
between rails
New Jersey transit
buses coughed
in the midnight air
(I felt wedged in commotion)
cursing teenagers
pissed in the alley-
way thurs., fri.,
and sat. nights
rock music reveille
from the snack shop
downstairs
kept me company
when John Lennon
died they played him
for months
finally
I awoke to silence
to the hush of thought
twanging in the a.m.
to the hollow beneath my throat
where a black-and-white accordion opened up

We left him behind

We left him behind *daddy daddy daddy*
because he didn't believe it

didn't believe we were going
to see her mother, her sister

Muskogee, Oklahoma
and the house where she was born

We packed potato salad, fried chicken
and left singing ninety-nine

bottles of beer on the wall.
her angels guided us, the ones

she saw when she went to the credit
union, the blond one she met once

on the steps at work, her angel teeth
upside down and smiling benignly.

We were guided like spiritual freight
swooped through New Mexico, Texas

Arizona.   When we returned
to California they left

Our house smelled stale
furniture clothed in sheets

behind us the Grand Canyon
the black night that swallowed us

outside Albuquerque, the dusty
rootbeer stands, the wooden-sided

station wagons with kids-blankets-
water jugs   all behind us

She gave me an enema, accused him
of turning our humble home

into a gambler's den while we were gone
Filling with water I screamed

at the fickleness of angels
who *never never never*

came to visit when we needed them
most   at home

Brown birds

The wrecking crew wrecks the factory
With every boom from the boom
Two finches on the street sign spring up
Alighting together every single time
On its dusty aluminum edge

Where can't they go, these delicate things
with their matching orange beaks and splotched wings?
Don't they know it will be months before
a whooping and hollering church will arise
With hundreds of shiny cars outside?

Gossips will call the deacons ex-drug dealers
Bigger birds will drop nastier notes
On each immaculate windshield
But today salvation sits on the bright
Orange beaks of two brown birds

The philosopher

Only two kinds of people
in this world-
daddy would grumble
as we walked
from the bus stop
and I pretended
my ankles were tied
forcing me to stumble
from lawn to lawn
-the caught and the uncaught

When my pretty catholic cousins
became pregnant
at fifteen
he handcuffed
the tiny yellow
babies into the family
I walked them
in endless circles
while the parents
went bowling
or to work

When my sister took her turn
at sixteen
he nearly bellowed
the baby out of her
promising to kill the boy
Rocking on her belly
scabbed by turpentine
she pleaded: don't hurt
him, it was half and half

When doctors needled fluid in
to catch my mistake
he would not hear
talk of first
and second
trimesters
psychiatrists
evaluating
my state of mind
He looked at
the gray gown
the male orderly
my dangling leg
as if he was helplessly ill

Later he said
he only wanted me to have
healthy babies
one day

Abortion he never talked about

The all-woman woman

I wear sensible shoes
sprout intelligent pimples
at my temples

Lick prune filling from hamentosh
doubt biographers whose
reconstructs move me yet
in cursive flight patterns

Bathe in a clawfoot tub
listen underwater to circa 1910 pipes
clanging the toilet habits of
my neighbors at periodic intervals

Feed pizza crust to plump duck freeloaders
stretch back to Sunday drivers
unused to their flat stares

Find fresh fears thumbing the concordance
varicose veins when
I kneel in reverence

Open my mail breathless as tongue kissing
find my checks every month bring on
my period

Massage my thighs stroking my self
softly pull nipples to hard ripple cord come
after checking for lumps

Dust wicker baskets
pardon my voyeur of necessity

study the she-vivid culture within
my windowed craving

Silk-screen the inadmissible
bowtied man at my groin
run dustballs from psychic
ruminations into the vacuum
hang my wardrobe of
hopehung skeletons
in my dark closet
to age   protected

Found poem from Sara

I buy black
shop black
shoot girl I even go all the way to fourteenth street
to see a black dentist
subway stops right there
my gynecologist is a black man
I take my clothes to a black cleaners
patronize black merchants
subscribe to essence, black enterprise
can't hack ebony, sorry bout that
lemme see
I have a black hairdresser
uh
he's gay?
love black theatre
if they'd ever start on time
I don't know what all the fuss is about
I like giving my money to black people
… I'll probably marry a white man

Weaning

Once an open-legged woman, best remembered
for being idle and infrequent, for leaving
her pride in sugar canisters
and forgetting the little

unnecessaries she left behind: double-
double locks, whatever you say, coarse
toenail stubs, histrionics,
potsherds and shoe heels

At another juncture, she would be fit
for collage, her spine stuck with binder's glue
but an instinct, her love
of fresh bread, leads her

on. Like a grain of wheat, she fords
the sieve, foregoing an arm sliced at the crook
Her inners go for embryonics
mouth to pieceputty

The devil faces a battle to forge his workshop
here. There are advantages: lonely women
the married, forsaken kind
seek her out.   She gives

them eye-to-eye contact
Like ship to ship
they become for one for all
deciphering from hollow to hollow

drawing strength from the flotilla
of drowned womanbodies
hairless, departed from the chattel
grimacing at the sun

smiling only in front of the full moon
which draws them close in profile
Occasionally their shoulders shrug
the torsos let out sighs

the habits of the nuptial remain
for open-legged women
not a one
any color other than roasted brittle

Their pumped navels sprout
a common flag of intercoursing
reflecting clear skies
in copula with the rainbow

for one for all
buoys of the whistle's antipodes
feeding their punctured *if*
you say so to the sea

mermaid mother me

as child is father of the man
a mermaid mothered me

a mermaid child fed my womanmind
made murmuring blue pleas sing
and slickened nature's slime

her gilled spirit harboured rocks' ripple
flow through spin-spun tides
dipping deep into dark ocean draughts
for a lived lifestream

the path of her moving was mood mine new
and touched over, a palm-held life
in stills of arctic night

mermaid mothered me
turned my legs to one sealed fin
beckoned my not-selves
to the feast from shrimp shells
and sea slug pots

amid the fathoms, soundings
buried gold and silver, I
crave gumbo over rice

and may grow old for the
brine in my orifice and
seaweed strapping my crotch

shafting light questions
over mermaid's slough,
feigning the cycle, scraping

tunnel crawlings, shouting
doomy proverbs to passing
seahorse pirates

o mermaid's pulse
saltspring a bled nipple tune
steep this girlsong sung
to a womanwrung chant

affinity

night has its way absolute with me
pervading my vision
off the highway
to trees on the side
of the road
lusting for spring in stoic
naked trance while
night's black beauty
seduces dusk rose
from a seedling sky

abuse here is natural and
foreordained

the one thing dissolved in the lengthening
the sun's
round face
as the highway lights up
with headlights
and a hundred houses
peer through gangly
trees
their bedrooms filled
with turned
on light. this
is my greed
wanting to be in the bedroom
the one bedroom in each house
lining the highway
with needs and desires
thrusting its lamplighted haven
onto my path

enticing a part of me
an alice-becoming part of me
to the rabbithole
for the swallowing
into the bedroom
a glance down a deepwell
remote as australia lined with colonials tudors
splits georgia pines redwood
littered with barbecues stairs bunkbeds
familyrooms knottypine
tall whitemen padding around
in slippers shedding fuzz
as balled up as this curious greed
sleeveless sweatervested whitemen clearing out
basements crammed with peeling white lawnswings
pipepuffing whitemen benign and reclining
on barcaloungers reading warpoorstocksshocks
snowblowers reduced for quick springsale
sincerely fretful whitemen who missmourn
citystreets and crowded traffic
straightbacked whitemen never out of
money out of work some on the verge
of suicide parking chrysler sedans
in two-car garages
monolithic whitemen with snowshovel
hatchets hanging from abominable backs
brutes to my naked eye
in this primordial spring
aging whitemen hungry over formica
counters shined by spittle
from this voracious need
huge nonsensical whitemen

dwarfing wifekidsdogscats
colorless absurd whitemen
looming over roomshalls
floorswallsdoors standing
gargantuan overwhelming
plank porches bigger than
paul bunyan staring past the
trees to the car
weaving in the distance
with my womanhead
swerving in the driver's seat
weighted by this wishlanguage
this fantasy of deprivation
steering the wheel of my eye
off the highway
past the trees
whistling soft as premature spring
on the lighted surface of evening

which summons this need
this what I want
so long past where it began
pure clear pelting my face
fresh as rain
taking me across these windowsills
where I perch
my eyes greedier than stout birds
swallowing escaped air
as if the momentary life I live
off this busy highway
depends on it

On the eve

−January 15, 1991
the eve of the Persian Gulf war

Last night I awoke with music in my head
       when johnny comes marching home again
I saw the boys coming home
Their bodies didn't match their heads
but they were marching and intact
their heads on Frankenstein-style
jagged stitches in the neck
smiling and intact

The men in my dream were white,
in fact, with famous comics' faces
a stitched-together Chevy Chase
Ted Danson with his neck in a brace

It was a 4:43 a.m. awakening
the time when either the spirit
or the bladder needs release
The dream women were Arab
and unveiled in bed
with heads but no bodies
eating pork sausages
puffing away on American cigarettes
and the music not jazz or sweet Brazil
not rhythm-and-blues or blues

My dream people chose their own music
and I can hear it now
when johnny comes marching home again
hooray hooray
when johnny comes marching home again
hoorah hoorah

We know

We know about terrorism
sometimes eat it
for breakfast lunch & dinner

It don't jet in
out of clear blue skies
every 60 years

We know
discrimination
segregation
hate crimes
hollywood
jim crow
lynching
slavery
hostility
redlining
profiling
last hired
first fired
stereotyping
birth of a nation
structural violence
justifiable homicide

Why do they hate us?
I never hear black people say this

Ballad for Sarah Palin's babymommadrama

Before anybody
politically right of center
says one word of defense
for this sweet young pale
pretty girl, can we hear
a disclaimer? Goes like this:

We regret demonizing whole
generations of young black
unwed females (not pale nor
considered pretty by white
ethnocentrics). We regret
stereotyping them
as immoral dregs on public
welfare rolls. We apologize
for forgetting that
sexuality is human
not racial
and that teen pregnancy
happens in the "best of
homes" (back in the day as well) and
before we did away with welfare
& forced these mothers into
minimum wage jobs two and three
bus rides away from their little
not-pale children (I believe you
called them bastards but we
invented better terms-
babymomma, babydaddy- that I know
all about because I'm not just
a grandma, I'm a babydaddymomma)
and the kids left all day

to watch TV and play video
games unsupervised. That's
what we call the bootiful
Clinton legacy. That's why
some very stoopid people
mistook Bill for a black prez

But that's so 80s/90s
Let us return to late 2008
when fair virgins of the
almost-no-longer-majority
race get impregnated mysteriously
and became upright political footballs

Let's let bygones be bygones and
remember the golden-white rule-
when people of color do it, it's evil,
when whites do it, it's a badge of honor

For Reggie Lockett
(1948-2008)

I'm just so mad that you up and left
without so much as a moment's notice
come to think of it when we met
we were mad   angry young poets at sf state
Madly in awe of the revolution
deliriously mad and happy to be reading sonia leroi
don lee sarah webster fabio askia marvin x ed bullins
mad at the world
mad at white people
mad at the system
mad at inequality
mad at the black bourgeoisie
mad mad mad mad mad
at all the madness around
us inside of us ahead of us
I'm glad we were there

Not everyone was too high to recall it
Some of us were too mad not to recall it
the madness our strike at repression
some said our finest
some said our worst
so what? We were mad!

Now the road has forked. You split
Carrying your leather bags into the beyond
I'm still sadgladmadcrazymad
That we blossomed
once in a seldom season
Like bellyflowers
that people have to get down
on their bellies to see

I can't run into you at a reading
So I will rail atop the sf-oakland bay bridge:
goodbye brother goodbye friend my mad mad friend

Goodbye

To Mrs. Lindella Goosby, a letter poem

To Mrs. Lindella Goosby
18th and Fondulac, Muskogee, Oklahoma

> *From Mrs. Florence Stapleton, Columbus, Georgia*
> *On the date of the fourth of June*
> *In the year of our Lord nineteen hundred and twelve*

Dear Lindella June

Please give Ma Goosby my kindest regard – She is not as you say
Adding salt to the wound – This blow has hit you an her equally hard

But I hear your heart bleating like a lost sheep across the windy plains
As to this so-called Rev Cleophus – Ma Goosby did write

Accusing you – Of taking an improper liking to him
Trust her in this matter – Circuit preachers can preach the gospel

Good as any man in a pulpit – But roaming is their habit
A womans heart an the prairie – Near bout equal to them

The very fact of him saying to Ma Goosby – What he never say to you
She a little piece of leather but she well put-together

Show he have less on his mind – An more round his holster
Than is good for him or yall – He sound liken a dip over here

An dip over there type – Iffen I read Ma Goosby right
You still young even with death – Having sat down

Inside your heart – Trust Ma Goosby as I do
For these two God honest reasons – She is blood to your child

She been through an through the storms of life
She can also iron up a petticoat stiff as you please

An thats an accomplishment Lindella darling
Men be like found money – If you find a shiny dollar on the street

Spend it dont depend on it – And dont be expecting to find it
Again – Sometime colored women happen up on mens

Like found money – You know what Poppa John used to say
White folks do business colored folk make rangements

Sometime what else can we do? Anybody you decide to get
A hold of Lindella – please remember

Here for the day gone for the morrow
We trying hard as bees in a bonnet to keep

Your heart from breaking again – A body can only take so much
Our preacher said death is a natural necessity

It must come to pass – MUST MEANS MUST
Keep the Good lord in your heart – Heep start but few goes

I am planning a late summer visit
Love, Mama

P.S. Preacher men is the hardest mens of all to live with
Has to keep his natural devil cooped up inside him

Let it out onliest in front of his wife and children
Even men with vices easier than a man of God~

canoe

*"I felt as if I had three hearts and they were so
large my body could hardly hold them."*
—Carl Sandburg's Sojourner Truth

my sojourner carrying
our lovely
ugly burden

welcome back
black hearted lilith
shelter me in myth

hike this precipice called breast
who needs three
to make it through?

your uncontaminated
pluck rocks
this canoe

Before and After

We stood on garbage cans to watch the assembly line
at the Chevrolet manufacturing plant on 73rd ave

> *See the USA in your Chevrolet*
> *America is asking you to call*
> *Drive your Chevrolet through the USA*
> *America's the greatest land of all*

We paid our parents no mind at all
when they said Dinah Shore was passing for white

Oakland had white-only garden apts. on 66th ave
housing UC Berkeley grad students
young dads in Bermuda shorts
moms in capri pants
a 99 year covenant kept us out
the little children called us *niggers*
if we took the shortcut home

Those apts. became the site of the 1980s drug wars
The would-be Coliseum was a swamp

> *BART was a developer's dream*
> *to bring suburban commuters to SF*
> *Oakland be damned*

We had to fight to get Oakland stops added
The boys across the street were from Georgia
Their mother welcomed my brother to peepee
in their bathroom but insisted he poopoo at home
I thought white people pooped white poops
And we pooped brown

Wave after wave of Ohlones, Mexicans, Chinese, Portuguese
Oakies and Arkies from the Oklahoma and Arkansas dust bowls
coloreds and whites from Louisiana, Texas and Oklahoma

migrated for munitions and troop movement work during WWII

Our parents and grandparents came in droves
planting their families and dreams
in the fertile soil called California

after

We're all Panthers now
The Black Panther Party did not backfire
It was an early warning system
for this entire country / world
about U.S. oppression
the ravages of imperialism
the rampant police-as-occupying-force
in the black community

As the vanguard it did exactly
what
it was historically tasked to do
it woke people up

What people choose to do now
under this near totalitarianism
is up to individuals and groups

We don't need Malcolm X, Marcus Garvey, Denmark Vesey
Harriet Tubman, Ida B. Wells-Barnett, Fannie Lou Hamer
MLK, John Lewis, Huey P. Newton, Eldridge Cleaver
Sojourner Truth, Rosa Parks, all our people
who fought to the finish

They came, they saw, they served
It's up to the living to stand up and be counted

I'm just saying

Imma be ok
Even wif lightening 'n thunder
setting de trees on fire
& dogs howling up a storm

but if I were a spooky sort
(which I is deep down)
I'd say we is coming into
de apock-a-lips

Acknowledgments

13th Moon
The bus terminal

The Aquarian Weekly Rock Magazine
Affinity

Asili
A place called California
canoe
In sickness and in health
Ballad for sarah palin's babymommadrama
Bruno was from Brazil

Bergen Poets Newsletter
at the cianci st. bar

Crab Orchard Review
To Mrs. Lindella Goosby [letterpoem]

Drumvoices Revue 2000
Oakland

Glint
The little girl
Today
The creek

Good News
A place called California
Bruno was from Brazil: a prose poem
The tale [as the hounding tale]

Konch
Note to my younger self

Lips
Woman

New Verse News
Ballad for sarah palin's babymomma drama
Before and After
I'm just saying
Poem for the rest of us

Making Sense: A Guide to Sound Reasoning and Critical Thinking
A place called California

Obsidian II
Fragile the bond never tested by a hard pull

Painted Bride Quarterly
Momma love you yepper do

Paterson Literary Review
Parent
The philosopher
We left him behind
The word divorce

The Poetry Café (raintiger.com)
Bling
Advice to a young actor

Poetry Monthly.com
Bling

Rooms
Oakland
Old love
Poem for my other mother
San Pablo Avenue
Why our bridge never went up
The year

Talking Writing
Manhattan my ass, you're in Oakland

Turning a Train of Thought Upside Down
Bling [nominated for a Pushcart Prize 2012]

Winning Writers Newsletter April 2007
Bruno was from Brazil: a prose poem

Kirkus Reviews

Advance critique of Manhattan my ass, you're in Oakland

Juanita, an elder stateswoman of human rights in America, was editor-in-chief of the Black Panthers' newspaper in the late 1960s. Her experiences in Oakland, California, are chronicled in her much lauded, semiautobiographical novel, Virgin Soul (2013). A renowned novelist, poet, and playwright, she showcases her deft use of numerous styles of poetry and modified prose in her new book. Many of the pieces are set against the backdrop of rough-and-tumble Oakland while invoking the legacies and lessons of black poets like Dudley Randall and Langston Hughes. Permeated with themes of sexual and racial inequality, this collection of 50-plus pieces fittingly begins with a credo against toxic masculinity, conjuring the Greek figure of Lysistrata. Similarly sexually charged imagery is often featured throughout the volume. These subtle and not-so-subtle erotic performances juxtapose the viciously practical with the beautiful. A classically structured sonnet dissects how "brothers get ferocious when they fuck" while another poem includes the lines "softly pull nipples to hard ripple cord come / after checking for lumps." This isn't the only way the work subverts readers' expectations; the collection often injects bodily disgust or mental discomfort into the pieces to catch the audience off guard. A return home to the staleness of a father-run household is punctuated by a screaming enema. A humorous prose piece about the use of the n-word is made all the more unsettling by the fact that it's predicated on the death of a Latino man who should not have been uttering the slur in the first place. Keeping readers on edge like this is an effective tactic to drive home the importance of the subjects addressed. One poem considers men needing women to be their props a systemic issue. In another piece, the ethereal imagery of downtrodden egg- and worm-eaters' rising up to reach a dispassionate white angel remains striking in its symbolism.

With the exception of a heart-stirring eulogy for a lost friend, the book often feels the most personal in works that focus on religion. A piece dedicated to the author's shakubuku mother, the woman who introduced her to Buddhist nam-myoho-renge-kyo chanting, is a portrait of words that skillfully brings the person to life: "She looked like my real mother / thirty years back: their large lips ochre-beautiful petals blossoming beneath their loopy lidded eyes / ...her womanscent, / pussy-sharp in pungent spirals." This same passion can be as heartbreaking as it is wondrous, as in a piece about an ailing father, willing to chant with Juanita at home, who refuses to enter a San Pablo, California, temple as he nears the end. On the subject of Christianity, the volume is considerably more critical, calling out Roman Catholic hypocrisy and seeing Jesus in the legions of white homeless, begging and defecating in the streets. Modern and historical hallmarks of social justice are present throughout, from Donald Trump's rise and Harvey Weinstein's crimes to the acquittal of O.J. Simpson, Sarah Palin's "babymommadrama," and the Gulf War. The author champions the causes of Hurricane Katrina survivors and examines police victims and tragedies like the fatal shooting of Atatiana Jefferson in Texas.

Unsettling, important, and unforgettable poetry.

A Critique of "Bruno Was From Brazil" by Jendi Reiter

This unusual and provocative piece, "Bruno Was from Brazil" by Judy Juanita, crosses the boundaries of genre (appropriately for a poem about explosive cross-cultural interaction). An example of the fluid form known as the prose poem, which has become increasingly popular in literary journals, this piece would also work well as a slam poetry performance. Neither form can rely on line breaks to signify that the text is "poetic", forcing the author to pay closer attention to aural patterns and timing in order to give the piece the musical momentum and intensity of a poem. Writing prose poems, or reading one's work aloud, are both useful tools for free-verse poets to discover whether they are allowing line breaks to substitute for true poetic speech.

What exactly is a prose poem? This overview from the Academy of American Poets website notes: "While it lacks the line breaks associated with poetry, the prose poem maintains a poetic quality, often utilizing techniques common to poetry, such as fragmentation, compression, repetition, and rhyme." Juanita's poem fits this description, with its staccato sentences, its wide-ranging associative leaps between topics and varieties of diction (news reports, conversation, academese and slang), and especially its mesmerizing repetition of That Word.

"Bruno Was from Brazil" initially leans toward the prosy side of the equation, beginning in the voice of a hard-boiled detective story: "I'm from Oakland and I'm not a statistic. Yet." Halfway through, somewhere around the line "Certain words are like gods," the piece takes off as a manic riff on racially charged language and whether its sting can ever be dulled by context. Without line breaks (brakes?), the words spill out furiously, defying decorum and step-by-step logic, so that when we finally reach the author's satirical "solution" of a constitutional amendment, it's obvious that we'll never be able to draw neat lines separating safe from dangerous uses of the word. In this way, the author's chosen form enhances the message and emotional impact of her story.

The hybrid poetic form liberates Juanita to include sentences that would feel too wordy and technical in a traditional lyric poem (particularly the section from "Forget Dick Gregory's autobiography" to "Our Nig"). Other sentences, by contrast, display more of the aphoristic, non-literal qualities of poetry: "now you know the last word in the guidebook for new arrivals is nigger"; "Stopped using the word and used crack instead"; and the passage "Certain words are like gods. They command respect. Nigger is a god. I'm so sorry for Bruno. He was a sacrificial lamb—that's what you have to do with gods. You have to appease them, give them a lil' somepin somepin."

The repetition of the word "god" parallels the subsequent variations on "nigger", reinforcing the connection between these concepts. Gods are lethally unpredictable, a power that we try and fail to contain with words and rituals, and yet a power we can't resist invoking to make sense of our lives. This poem suggests that racial and cultural identity, and perhaps even language itself, are essential aspects of being human, but also have the potential to dehumanize. Where there are borders, there will be wars.

The latter half of the poem seems to deride academic efforts to domesticate the word, implicitly questioning whether this is just another way of encouraging children to play with live ammunition. The line between safe and unsafe contexts is easy to cross unawares; wouldn't it be better to suppress the word entirely? On the other hand, how can we think and speak critically about real and persistent racial divisions if we allow racist language to silence us? Neither speech nor silence can perfectly preserve the illusion of a vantage point outside the moral failures of our culture. By choosing to use the word—to rub our noses in it, in fact—but ending with a self-mocking non-solution, Juanita makes us see that cosmetic changes to language only conceal racism, not eliminate it.

Adding to the moral ambiguity, "nigger" is a word traditionally used by whites to oppress blacks, but the homicide victim in this poem is a Latino immigrant who used the word in ignorance, and his assailants are African-American. Who is truly innocent here? The shooters, or men in their social world, might have felt they were resisting oppression by putting a positive spin on a word that the white majority used against them (the way some gays have reclaimed "queer"), but clearly the word still hurts them, no matter how tough they try to become by using it on each other. It's like keeping a loaded gun in your house: all it takes is one curious child to turn responsible self-defense into irresponsible risk.

Some interesting postmodern themes that arise in this piece: "Bruno Was from Brazil" is a poem about language that points to its own inadequacy, yet cannot be silent. It's also about the disjunction between signifier and signified. Repeat a word often enough and it starts to sound strange, almost nonsensical. Abstracted from its interpersonal context, the word as word reveals itself to be empty, arbitrary. Yet this can lull us into a false sense of security, because of course the interpersonal context is always there, and the word in the real world always has a history and an explosive charge. The author, the speaker, is not in complete control of how the word will be received. Is it "just a word"? Yes—and no.

Reprinted by permission of Jendi Reiter. http://winningwriters.com/resources/bruno-was-from-brazil.

About the Author

Judy Juanita is a novelist, poet, playwright and essayist whose focus is the peculiar paths trodden by black people in the Golden State, black politics, culture and art, and California's vigor and culture.

Her book of essays, *De Facto Feminism: Essays Straight Outta Oakland* [EquiDistance, 2016], explores key shifts and contradictions in her own artistic development as it explores black and female empowerment. It was a distinguished finalist in OSU's 2016 Non/Fiction Collection Prize. The poem "Bling" in this collection was nominated for a Pushcart Prize as was her essay, "The Gun as Performance Poem."

Her semi-autobiographical debut novel, *Virgin Soul* [Viking, 2013], features a young woman in the 60s who joins the Black Panther Party. Her collection of short stories, "The High Price of Freeways," is a three-time finalist in the Livingston Press Tartt Fiction Award; stories from the collection appear in *Oakland Noir, Crab Orchard Review, The Female Complaint, Imagination & Place: an anthology, Tartt Six and Tartt Seven.*

At SFSU, as an undergrad, she joined The Black Panther Party In 1967 alongside her college roommates. From his jail cell, Huey Newton appointed her editor-in-chief of the party's newspaper in 1968. That year, she joined fellow SF State student protestors in an historic 4-1/2 month strike which revolutionized American higher education and created the nation's first black studies department. She was the editor-in-chief of the strike journal, Black Fire. After graduating with a B.A. in psychology in 1969, she became the youngest member of this new department, teaching black psychology and black journalism. In 2019, a play of hers at Beyond Baroque in L.A., "Life is a Carousel," pits a black woman academic against the forgotten founder of Black Studies about the academy, Black Studies and the struggle. This play is included in Juanita's book *Homage to the Black Arts Movement: A Handbook* (EquiDistance, 2018). Juanita's twenty-odd plays have been produced in the Bay Area, L.A. and NYC.

CPSIA information can be obtained
at www.ICGtesting.com
Printed in the USA
FSHW022230301220
77292FS